Hillerman, Tony.
Indian country

NDIAN COUNTRY

INDIAN COUNTRY
America's Sacred Land

Text by Tony Hillerman
Photographs by Béla Kalman

YEAROUT EDITIONS • WESTON, MASSACHUSETTS

Cover: Ceremonial dancers descend into their kiva after a St. Francis ritual at Nambe Pueblo; in the background are the snowcapped Sangre de Cristo Mountains, landmark of the "Middle Place" of the Nambe Universe and home of the kachina spirits.

Photographs copyright © 1987 by Béla Kalman
Text copyright © 1987 by Tony Hillerman
All Rights Reserved
Third Printing 1992
ISBN 0-87358-432-5 softcover
ISBN 0-87358-428-7 hardcover
Library of Congress Catalog Card Number 86-46375

Library of Congress Cataloging-in-Publication Data

Hillerman, Tony.
   Indian country.

    1. Indians of North America–Southwest, New.
2. Southwest, New–Description and travel–1981–
Views. I. Kalman, Bela. II. Title.
E78.S7H65 1987 979'.00497 86–46375
ISBN 0–87358–428–7
ISBN 0–87358–432–5 (pbk.)

Preface

I*ndian Country, America's Sacred Land,* is my tribute to the Southwest. A few years ago, a painter friend of mine from Boston moved to Nambe in New Mexico. He urged me to come and see this uniquely different part of the United States, an area little known by Easterners. Our next vacation was spent in Santa Fe, New Mexico, travelling by car and small plane all over the region. After that three week trip, I knew I was hooked.

We built a house outside of Santa Fe and I use it as a base camp for my photography. Indian Country stretches from Santa Fe to Flagstaff, Arizona, and from Alamogordo, New Mexico, to Bryce Canyon, Utah. The sharp colors in this book are the result of extreme visibility and crisp light. The unusual shapes, the rare symmetry of patterns and serene majesty of nature are present everywhere. One doesn't need an eagle's eye to see it, but one needs a very fast finger on the shutter to catch these fleeting images.

I believe that a photographer with many decades of visual training develops a third eye, and this third eye, in conjunction with the other two, sees beyond the range of physical vision. These photographs zoom in and out of history, showing the Southwest of a millennium ago as well as of today, from the air and from the ground. The spiritual richness I encountered in my ten years of search for wordless beauty turned my curious eye into a loving one. Work became pleasure, and the sacred land became my Garden of Eden.

I want to express my profound appreciation to William Field, Ike Kalangis, Dickie Pfaelzer, Tony Hillerman and my dear wife Edna Kalman for their help and advice in this labor of love.

Béla Kalman
May 1992

INDIAN COUNTRY
America's Sacred Land

The westbound Amtrak left Albuquerque a little later than usual that day. It hurried south through the cottonwood bosque of the Rio Grande to Isleta and then made the slow curving climb westward, up the hill toward the Rio Puerco breaks. In the observation car, three men were engaged in one of those easy conversations that train trips provoke among strangers. The man who had boarded at Chicago was telling the man from Hartford and the man from St. Louis about an eccentric woman in his office. The train topped the ridge. The vastness of western New Mexico opened before us, the fierce sun slanting toward the northwestern horizon. Noer Butte, Chicken Mountain, the Cebollitos and the Zunis range were cut off from their bases by the heat-haze of the afternoon. Mount Taylor seemed to have slipped free of the magic knife with which the Navajo First Man had pinned it to the earth and floated on its own shimmering mirage. One thunderstorm brewed over Chivato Mesa. Another was

The mechanics of pump irrigation
force wheat fields into circles in the
San Luis Valley near Alamosa,
Colorado. The mechanics of biology
draw the trunks of aspen into vertical
white lines in the Taos Mountains.

*Time's chemistry converts the barren
hills of Death Valley into a geometry
of lines at Zabriskie Point . . .*

. . . to be repeated by the earth-moving machinery in the Santa Rita Mine near Silver City, New Mexico . . .

. . . and repeated again on the loom of the Navajo weaver in a rug in Hilda Street's collection in Santa Fe . . .

. . . and again in B-52 bombers stored at Davis Monthan Air Force Base outside Tucson, Arizona.

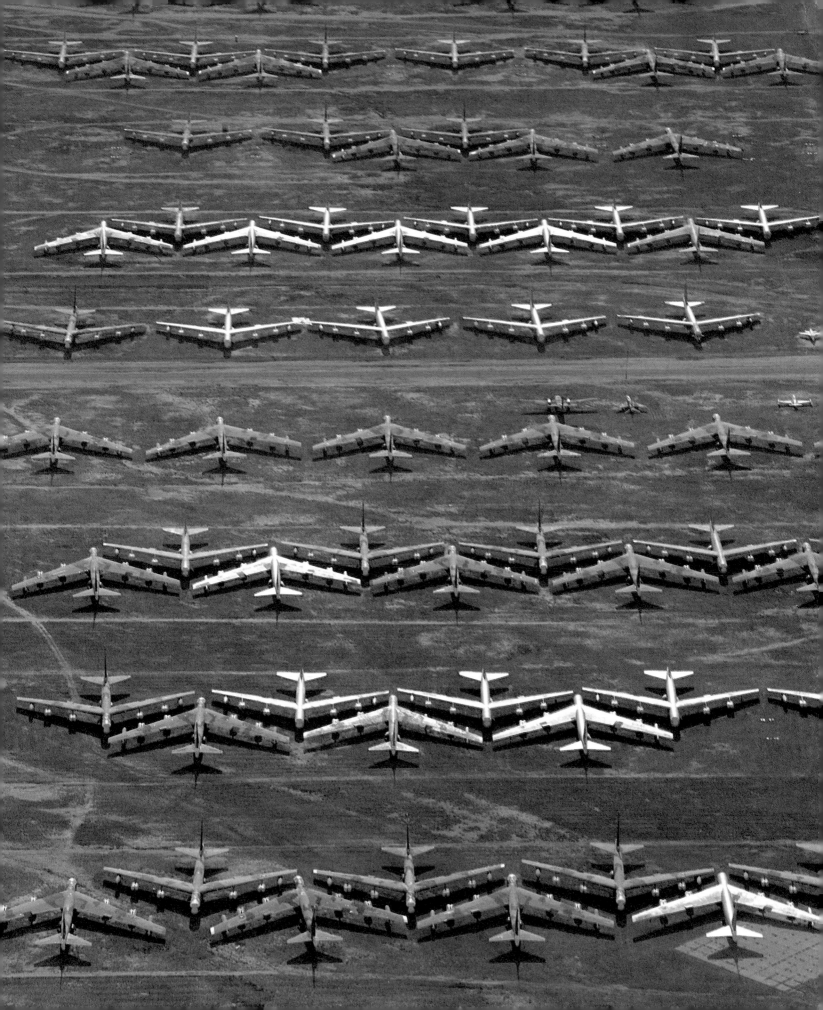

In the Shidoni Sculpture Park at Tesuque, New Mexico, Edwin Rivera's interpretation of totem offerings suggest the pahos *made by the Pueblo kiva fraternities, and the prayer sticks of the Navajo shamans . . . offerings to the spirits against an almost empty sky.*

At the museum of the White Sands Missile Range, the antique rockets that pioneered man's journey to the moon stand against a Father Sky decorated by the vapor trails of jets.

At Yellowstone, Mother Earth vents her warmth in plumes and creates an atmosphere of mist.

*Above the Santa Clara Pueblo, an X of
vapor trails marks The Middle Place
of the World. Here the mythic Long
Sash led the Tewa people in their
migration from the Land of Long
Darkness to the Rio Grande Valley.*

building north of the Jemez range. Before us stretched an infinity of prairie—tan, grey, silver and yellow, punctuated with a rare juniper and dappled with cloud shadows. Beyond these dry steppes rose the serene blue mountains. It is a view that always jolts me out of my urban preoccupations, separates me from my troubles, lifts my spirits, fills me with a sort of joy.

In the observation car, the conversation died mid-sentence.

"My God!" the man from Hartford exclaimed. "Why would anyone live out here?"

Why, indeed.

Viewed objectively, it is a harsh and hostile landscape. In fact, none of this vast territory which Easterners once called "The Great American Desert" offers much to the pragmatic person with materialistic values. Westward from the New Mexico-Texas border, all

Far down the Rio Grande, snow geese (modern migrants from Long Darkness country) swarm into the sky over the Bosque del Apache marshes. Sandhill cranes watch in the background.

To the west, across the Coyote Hills and the San Mateo Mountains in the emptiness of the Plains of San Augustin, the immense radio-telescopes of the National Radio Astronomy Observatory mimic a V of geese. But these Very Large Array "telescopes" are not wings, but ears. They listen to the sounds from the Milky Way —the tracks that Long Sash and his people followed down the sky.

across the southern Rockies, the Colorado Plateau and the dry and eroded high country which finally slopes away toward California, there is little to appeal to man's yearnings for a fruitful land of milk and honey. Our Genesis, the Judeo-Christian story of creation, teaches that God said that Man should have "dominion over all this earth." But this country is hard to dominate. It is built too big for human convenience. It lacks the fertility that man values and the moderation that makes him comfortable. Something primal in even the most urbane citizen warns him of hunger and thirst out there beyond that train window, of merciless sun in the summer, cold in the winter, of a two-day walk to the nearest neighbor, of places where a person could die as easily as a field mouse. It puts man on a scale in which he is not comfortable—a tiny insignificant creature surrounded by emptiness.

Maasaw, the guardian spirit of this present world, warned the Hopis about it: to live here, they must be content without material comforts. In 1868, General William Tecumseh Sherman warned the Navajos — and told President Andrew Johnson that the people held captive at Bosque Redondo probably could not support themselves if allowed to return to the high desert country they called "Dinetah." But, since it was desolate, infertile and generally worthless, these Navajos should be safe there from the greed of white society. It was, General Sherman assured the president, "as far from our future possible wants as is possible to determine."

Their Origin Story tells us that when the Hopis emerged from their destroyed Third World into this Fourth World, they were met by Sotuknang, the supernatural being to whom God had given the job of creating the universe, and by Maasaw, who would be the Fourth World's guardian spirit. Sotuknang told them that this new world they would occupy was not like the easy and comfortable Third World that they had corrupted by their evil. While it, too, offered an easy life, it also offered heat and cold, height and depth, beauty and ugliness. The Hopis should choose the way of life that would be best for carrying out the role that God had given them. According to a related legend, Maasaw then offered the Hopis a choice of ears of corn. The Hopis selected a small, hard, durable ear. Thus they chose the tough, lean life where no possibility of material wealth could interfere with matters of the spirit.

Pepto Bismol® bottles, symbols of the Heartburn Age, form their linear pattern on a fence at Golden, New Mexico . . .

Would that explain to the man from Hartford why the Hopis elected, in an almost-empty world that was theirs for the asking, to live on the Hopi Mesas—a tough place to make a living?

That the Navajos made a similar free choice is a matter of public record, transcribed in the official minutes of the Peace Commission headed by General Sherman. More than seven thousand of them—all who had survived four dismal years in captivity at Bosque Redondo—were offered a treaty. In return for their promise to war no more, they could have a reservation in Oklahoma (a delegation had inspected it and found it fertile and well-watered, with lush grazing). Or they could have a reservation at Bosque Redondo, on the Pecos River where they had been held since 1863. Or they could return to the desolate Colorado Plateau where the army under their "friend," Colonel Kit Carson, had hunted them down, chopping down their orchards, burning their hogans, slaughtering their flocks, destroying everything in a successful effort to starve them into submission.

The Navajos conferred, then met with General Sherman. Barboncito, a war leader, was spokesman. He told Sherman he spoke not just for the Navajos but "for the animals, from the horse to the dog, and also for the unborn." Their decision, he said, was unanimous. They would go home.

. . . repeated by mailboxes which say that even the open spaces behind the mountains have their scattered occupants . . .

Wherever your eye falls on this landscape, it finds patterns. The ruins of
Fort Union, where once the Army
imposed order on a new land, form an
anachronistic shape on the high
prairie of eastern New Mexico . . . and
the old iron tracks of the Cumbres
and Toltec narrow-guage railroad add
their line of contrasting color to the
pattern of aspen, fir and spruce above
Chama . . .

. . . in places like the Pecos Valley, where snowmelt has fed patchwork fields of subsistence farmers for centuries . . .

. . . or at Nambe.

The patterns of flower petals are reproduced in streets of suburban Tucson . . . and in a village of mobile homes outside Santa Fe.

North, beyond Cumbres Pass and across the San Luis Valley in Great Sand Dunes National Monument, the wind has left its patterned print on the dunes north of Mount Blanco, the sacred Sisnajini of Navajo mythology.

The Navajo yei called First Man built this Mountain of the East, and decorated it with white abalone shells. Here live Rock Crystal Girl and Rock Crystal Boy and here, in the poetry of Navajo creation, the white doves nested.

But at City of Rocks State Park south of Silver City, the wind-sculptured boulders stand changeless under a sky white with dry weather clouds.

"I hope to God you will not ask us to go to any country but our own," Barboncito said. "Our grandfathers had no idea of living in any other place.... When the Navajos were first created, four mountains and four rivers were pointed out to us. That was to be our Dinetah and it was given to us by Changing Woman." This same supernatural Holy Person had created the first four Navajo clans from the skin of her bosom, Barboncito explained, and had created the land between the four sacred mountains especially for them. Barboncito told the general that their forefathers had taught them never to leave this Holy Land. Away from Dinetah, "whatever we do causes death." The Pecos River drowned them when they washed in it. Lightning killed them. Even their old friend, the rattlesnake, struck them here without warning.

And above Cochiti Pueblo, wind and water have spent thousands of years carving these tent rocks from the volcanic ash of the Pajarito Plateau.

Unlike the work of nature, the work of man lacks permanence. At Madrid, New Mexico, the sagging homes of coal miners are being reclaimed from their "ghost" status by the artists and craftspeople who are beginning to repopulate the town.

Golden, New Mexico, where a century of abandonment reduced the gold-miners' homes to stony shells, is also in the process of resurrection by artisans seeking the peace and inspiration of isolation.

Man is more abrupt. His work rose at Gran Quivera . . . and at the "Salt Pueblos" of Salinas Monument . . . and fell into ruins within a tick of geological time.

At Quarai (above) *and Abo* (right and next two pages), *civilization flourished for only a handful of generations. Now its rooms are roosts for owls.*

Bubonic plague, or perhaps the aftermath of the seventeenth-century Pueblo Revolt, emptied the great church and convent at Pecos.

On the Rio Grande, below the cliffs of the Pajarito Plateau, the Kachina spirits of the San Ildefonso people still occupy the shrines on Black Mesa (right).

"The mourning of our women makes the tears roll down into my mustache," Barboncito said. "I can think only of Dinetah. I am just like a woman, sorry like a woman in trouble. I want to go and see my own country."

The Hopis' legends tell them that they are tied to their high corner of desert by destiny; they are living out supernatural prophecies. God told them to make migrations to the ends of the earth, to find the Center of the Universe, and to live there until this Fourth World ends. They found this center, this "Tuwanasavi," at the south end of Black Mesa. There they will live into eternity. The same is true in varying ways of the other tribes who found their sacred places and built their Pueblo societies up and down the Rio Grande, and at Ácoma, Zuni, Laguna and elsewhere. In different ways it is true of the Navajos, as Barboncito explained to Sherman, and of the Apaches, held by their Mountain Spirits, and for the Utes, the Papagos, the Havasupais and all the others. For all of them, these first comers, this is the Holy Land.

But how about the rest of us? What about Béla Kalman, whose native land is Hungary, and me, born in Oklahoma, and the others to whom this landscape also represents more than mere geography? How do we answer the man from Hartford?

I have hunted for that answer since an August afternoon when my wife Marie and I stood beside our old Ford near Clayton, New Mexico, and experienced our first High Plains thunderstorm. The air, hot and humid across Texas, was suddenly cold and — for a flatlander — incredibly transparent. There was an artillery of thunder, a heady ozone smell, and a dazzling aftermath of rainbows that made the stormy sky luminous with color. It was 1950, and it took us two years to complete our migration to our own Tuwanasavi. But from that day we knew as well as Barboncito or the Hopi Bear Clan where we were intended to live.

In Frijoles Canyon, the cliff rooms once occupied by the forefathers of the Pueblo tribes offer visitors a look into the past.

The New England poet, Winfield Townley Scott, also came for a visit and found he couldn't leave. What is it about this part of America, Scott asked, "that has seized upon astonishing numbers of people who came to look, and then put down their luggage and remained?"

First of all, Scott decided, "the magic is in the land itself, the magnificent stretches and towers of land.... The breadth and height of the land, its huge self and its huge sky, strike you like a blow. There are those who at once dislike it; in a kind of dismay at so much inhuman space, they flee from it. There are more who at first can do nothing but stand and stare." Exactly. The man from Hartford is dismayed. But Béla Kalman and I see something that moves us. We stand and stare.

The magic is indeed in the land itself. The Hopi, Zuni, Navajo and the peoples who built their pueblos in the watershed of the Rio Grande have been here far longer than we. They have had time to formalize that magic. Their ancestors named its landmarks, personified its spirits, and explained it with mythologies as rich and complex as those our ancestors gave us from the rivers of Iraq, the mountains of Lebanon, the dark forests of northern Europe and the islands of Greece. The Navajo populated Shiprock, and places like it, with memories of Monster Slayer, Spider Grandmother, the Winged Monsters and their other metaphors for the human struggle to endure. But the magic is also there for those of us whose culture grows from the law of Moses instead of the teachings of Changing Woman. We also see in an old volcanic core like Shiprock a reminder of antiquity beyond our power to imagine and forces beyond our power to control. Such harsh inhospitable beauty reminds us that man is not as much master of his planet, or of his destiny, as he likes to think.

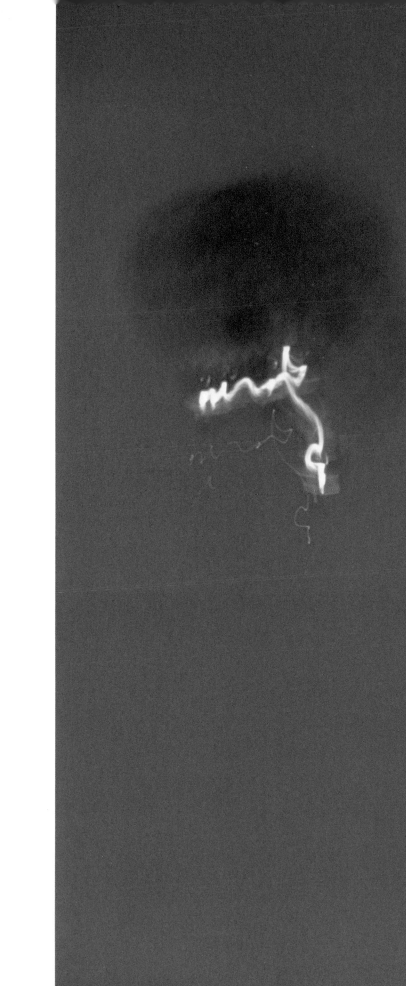

Hot air balloons competing in the Albuquerque International Balloon Festival add new color to the dark blue sky . . .

Those interested in the older cultures in this high, dry country learn its religious landmarks. Thus, when they see the San Francisco Peaks, Huerfano Mesa, Gobernador Knob, Corn Mountain or Zuni Salt Lake, these places communicate more than their physical presence. They stand as spiritual symbols — as do Mount Sinai, the River Jordan, the Wailing Wall or the Dome of the Rock. For this part of the Southwest is an American Holy Land. Its mythic sites remind us of humanity's drive to civilize itself, as do the landmarks of Israel and Greece.

Of all these landmarks my favorite is Mount Taylor, that exhausted volcano seventy miles west of Albuquerque. The Navajo call it "Tsoodzil," the Turquoise Mountain. It is the southern cornerpost of their *Diné Bikeyah*, the "Land Between the Mountains" outside of which their curing ceremonials cannot be performed. It was rebuilt in its present form in the Navajo Fifth World by the supernatural First Man, who brought up its materials from the drowned Fourth World. He spread a blue blanket on the ground, shaped the mountain, pinned it to the earth with a magic flint knife, decorated it with gems of turquoise, and assigned another "yei" from the Navajo pantheon of spirits, Turquoise Girl, to live on Mosca Peak, forever guarding the Navajo from the evils that might disrupt their harmony with the universe. There, in the poetry of the Navajo creation story, the bluebirds nest. And there the morning mist forms the holy House Made of Dawn.

. . . and perch like a cluster of Easter eggs awaiting takeoff.

Living in both hogans and more conventional structures, Navajo families fulfill their love of isolation at Los Gigantes south of Mexican Water (top), and near Roundrock.

Laguna Pueblo, dominated by its seventeenth-century mission church, stands in front of Tsoodzil, *the Turquoise Mountain, which First Man built as the home of Turquoise Girl. On our maps, it is called Mount Taylor, the old volcano overlooking Grants, New Mexico.*

*Steps that lead to the rooftop entrance
of San Ildefonso's kiva.*

*Viga shadows declare high noon at the
old Rio Grande pueblo of San Ildefonso.*

George Lopez, with one of his traditional bird carvings, and his niece Gloria Lopez at work on an effigy that will ride, with drawn bow, a death cart in a Lenten procession. The two Cordova carvers help make the northern New Mexico village a mecca for folk art collectors.

The Rio Grande Gorge bridge soars across the canyon between Taos and the village of Tres Piedras. The river tumbles over its narrow bed of boulders eight hundred feet below. Golden eagles nest in the cliffs, making it one of the few places man can look down on an eagle in flight.

Taos Pueblo was at least two hundred
years old when the Spanish explorer
Francisco Vasquez de Coronado saw it
in 1540. Its bakers cooked then as
now in outdoor beehive ovens called
hornos.

Oddly, the method of folding a blanket around the face, now traditional at Taos, is characteristic of a tribe on the Arabian Peninsula. One of those attracted to Taos when it was becoming a mecca for artists had been painting Bedouin tribesmen in North Africa. He showed his Taos models the Arab blanket fold and it quickly became Taos fashion.

The old Church of San Geronimo at Taos (right) was destroyed in 1847. Putting down a revolt by Taos Indians and neighboring villagers, the U.S. Army fired a cannon point-blank through a hole knocked in the church wall, killing its defenders and burning the building. The pueblo replaced it with the "new" church on the west side of the plaza.

I see this mountain every day from my window in northeastern Albuquerque. It looms on the western horizon, blue with distance. In what the Navajos call "The Season When Thunder Sleeps," it is whitecapped with snow. It wears a blowing scarf of clouds in the windy spring, and is the base of immense blue-black storm clouds when August brings the monsoon season to the southern Rockies. On days when Albuquerque's smog fills the Rio Grande Valley, the blue shape of the mountain seems to separate itself from the earth and float above the grey haze. On those rare occasions when curtains of rain drag across the Plain of Albuquerque and hide Tsoodzil, it is still in my mind, a memorized mountain. It changes with my mood: sometimes an indigo shape against the garish flare of sunset, sometimes a cold blue sawtooth on the horizon. But it always reminds me of the world of Navajo spirits.

In the Navajo version of mankind's Genesis, it was on this Turquoise Mountain that Monster Slayer and Born for Water, twin sons of Changing Woman, killed the giant called Ye-itso with magic arrows of lightning stolen from the Sun. Thus began their odyssey to make Diné Bikeyah safe for human occupation. The monsters infesting the Navajo Holy Land were products of disharmony with nature. First Man and First Woman had quarreled, defied natural law and attempted life without the opposite sex — a process that produced monsters which were destroying humanity. Their poetic stories of the conquest of the monsters are the Navajo metaphor for salvation — of human ability to transcend unhealthy appetites that disrupt the harmony of the Navajo Way.

People of Picuris dance in the pueblo's plaza, re-enacting the story of how they first obtained corn.

At Tesuque Pueblo, (next three pages)
dancers perform Los Matachines, a
ceremonial in which their own pueblo's
customs are combined with a folk
ritual imported from medieval Spain.

The Spanish and Native American cultures meld in many ways in the Southwest. The massive pueblo form of the St. Francis of Assisi church (at right, *its window decorated for Christmas*) at Ranchos de Taos combines architectural elements from Moorish Spain and the native pueblo form.

Entrances, at Ranchos de Taos (left)
and the old mission church at Picuris
Pueblo.

The Santuario at Chimayo (left, exterior) was originally built in the nineteenth century as a family chapel. Legends of miraculous cures have made it the goal of pilgrimages and of the prayerful and penitential visits of thousands every year.

The Church of San Jose de Gracia (left) *at the tiny village of Las Trampas is considered by antiquarians the most perfect surviving example of Spanish Colonial chapels. It was started in 1750 and completed about thirty years later.*

Tajique cross.

Spanish Colonial folk art at the Millicent Rogers Museum in Taos. The museum houses a superb collection of the very best Indian and Spanish American art.

Those whose prayers are answered leave momentos of their cures and their pilgrimages in the Santuario (left).

*Cottonwood skeleton and sky near
Taos.*

At the old gold town of Golden, a restored Franciscan chapel.

Near Dixon (left), a memorial to the spirit.

*Crosses of rough wood mark
pilgrimages completed at a shrine
near Santa Fe . . . and crosses of
aluminum and steel mark a storage
dump for used aircraft at Davis
Monthan Air Force Base outside
Tucson.*

Whether or not we can connect its landmarks to our own theology, it seems to me that this empty landscape speaks in its way to many of us. It has given me my own list of special places and I know many others who can say the same. For Norman Zollinger, it is the Carrizozo Basin of south-central New Mexico. He first saw it as a bombing range when he was an air force trainee in World War II, and returned to use it as a setting for his novels. Oliver LaFarge based his Pulitzer Prize first novel on the Navajos, but his heart lay in the impoverished Mora valley. For poet-essayist Haniel Long, the sacred places were all around. Long remembered the kosharis dancing for rain in the plaza of Cochiti Pueblo, and the rain falling, blurring the ceremonial black-and-white stripes with which members of this sacred fraternity decorate their bodies. He remembered a koshari falling, cutting his hip, ignoring the pain, drinking the rain from his hands—jubilant. Years later, Long wrote: "That koshar[i] is a living frieze in my mind. He multiplies himself into incomparable figures against the green of river trees, against sheet lightning lighting the hills." And of Cienega he wrote:

> I see it all again; and yet, can those houses be so red? And the dogs the children play with, can they be so white? And the Cerrillos Hills seen through an arroyo leading skyward, can they be so blue? Perhaps Cienega is an enchantment. And when one goes to it between the walls of blue rock, one may really not be going to it at all, but rather dreaming a dream he has dreamt before. Surely no one can be certain he has visited Cienega; people say to themselves, do they not: "Was it a vision; or have I at some time or another seen dusk in a valley like this?"

For many of us, other places in this high, dry, clear-aired country seem to engrave themselves on the memory like the rain on Cochiti Plaza and twilight at Cienega. My own memory is rich with very personal sacred places.

Gypsum leached from the Organ Mountains is formed into waves by the wind at White Sands National Monument. Rain congeals it, sun cracks it and the moving air carves its sculptured forms.

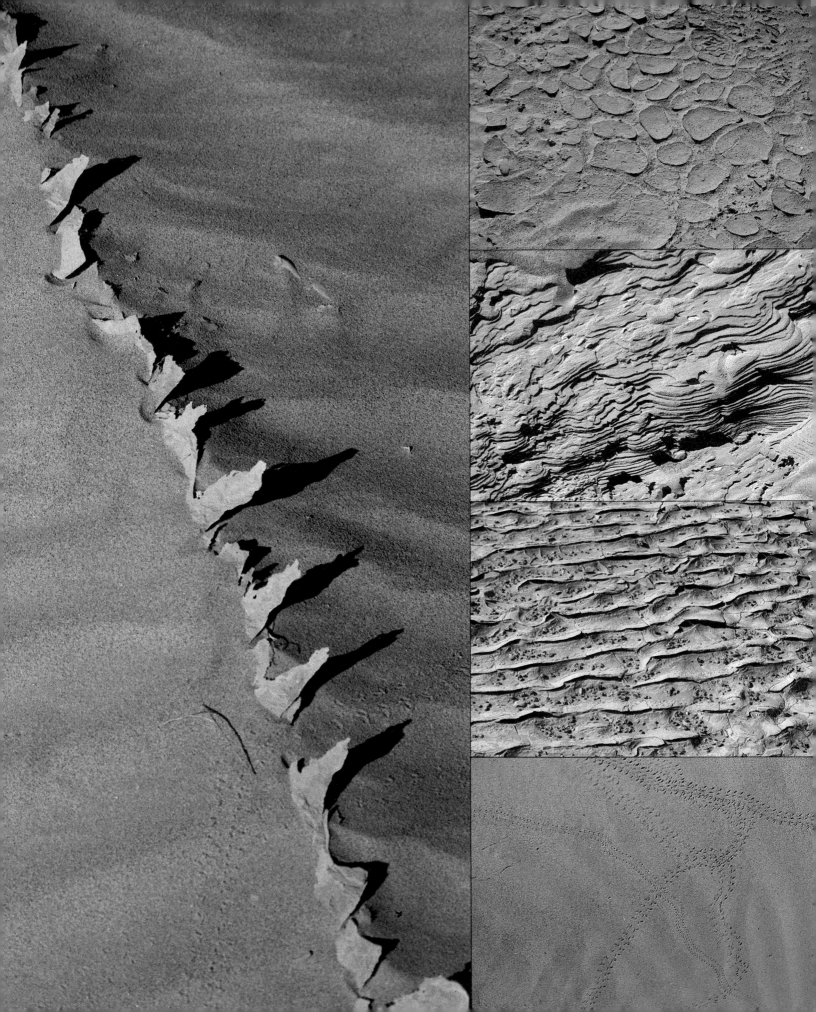

At White Sands on a cold winter night, the gatehouse is deserted, the access road is as empty as if only my car had ever existed. The night is windless. The moon is down but starlight reflects off the snowbanks in the San Francisco Mountains and the San Andres range. Far to the north, Sierra Blanca seems to glow. The odd squeak of my shoes on the cold gypsum is the single sound in a universe as silent and empty as Antarctica. A few hundred yards from the road, footprints on the white dunes are the only evidence of life on the planet.

Therapists try for something like this effect of utter isolation by immersing patients in body-temperature water and leaving them cut off from light and sound. They call it sensory deprivation. But at White Sands on a winter midnight, you attain the isolation without the deprivation. No light is visible from highway or window, but the sky is adazzle with stars—illumination enough to find your way through a wilderness of dunes. If you climb one and stand at its crest, you see whatever your imagination, and your mood, suggests. You can see the terrible loneliness of the planet's only survivor, or the incredible beauty that Maheo, the All Powerful Creator of the Cheyenne, built into the planet when he formed it on his palm; or, in the symmetry of dune-shapes and windlines, and the subdued starlight colors, inspiration for an abstract painter.

Across the Tularosa Basin, in view of this old lake bed, is a ridge where early hunters camped to watch for game. They covered the boulders there with abstract petroglyphs, many of which suggest the work of Klee and Picasso. Some spirit in this place spurs man to create beauty.

Ácoma Pueblo, the "Sky City" that the Ácomans and their Zuni allies tried unsuccessfully to defend from the Spanish conquistadores in the seventeenth century, stands mostly empty now, occupied only by a few families who guide tourists and sell their famous black-on-white Ácoma pottery. The village competes with the Hopis' Oraibi as the oldest continually occupied site in the United States.

Early summer is the best season to experience another of the places that always seem to speak to me. The place is the Taos Plateau, the ancient sheet of lava which, eons ago, filled the valley between the Taos Mountains in the Sangre de Cristos and the Brazos Range to the west. Later eruptions buried it under layers of ash and built their cinder cones here and there, and the Rio Grande sliced its great black gorge through it. Early summer is the best season because that is the peak of the runoff, when snowmelt from Colorado's high country roars down the river. And the best time is twilight on one of those days when clouds form over the Sangre de Cristo range and reflections from the setting sun color them red. Drive southward toward Taos from Tres Piedras on Highway 64. Pull off the road before you reach the Taos Gorge bridge. Walk out into the

A settlement of Mogollon farmers built the cliff dwellings of the Gila National Monument above the valley of the Gila River about 1280. They grew corn, beans and squash in the fields below for less than forty years, then vanished. No one knows why, or to where.

universe of sage, chamisa, snakeweed and gramma that covers the plateau. When the pavement is out of sight behind you, stand and look and listen.

You see what Frederick Remington saw when he rode across this plateau in 1882 enroute to Taos — a sort of beauty the famous painter of the frontier West never forgot. You are seven thousand feet above sea level here and the thin, transparent air seems to destroy distance. On the eastern horizon, Pueblo Peak and Lew Wallace Mountain glow red, pink and salmon in the garish sunset. Behind them is Blue Lake, Holy of Holies to the Taos Indians and the door between the worlds for their kachina spirits. The conical shape of Ute Mountain rises to the north. There the shamans of the Utes communed with God before Comanche, and Spanish, and finally white settlers drove them out of this great valley and across the Rockies. The dim outline of Mount Blanca is on the horizon beyond Ute, a feature of the Sangre de Cristo Range. The Navajos call it *Sis Naajini*, or White Shell Mountain, and it is one of the magic cornerposts of their world. The story of their origin tells us that First Man spread a white blanket on the earth and built Mount Blanco just as he built Mount Taylor. Here lives the spirit, Dawn Boy, who welcomes beauty into the land of the Navajos. And with him lives Shash, the magic bear, guarding the people from evil.

Through the crystalline air, these landmarks are etched against the background sky, looking close enough to reach in minutes. The sage stretches endlessly toward the mountains, apparently seamless, showing no visible sign of the great river that has cut its canyon through it.

But listen! On this windless evening you hear something strange and indefinable. It seems to come from far away, something like endless thunder. It seems to come from the earth itself, an eerie sound. You know you are hearing the river, the distant sound of a billion tons of water falling, crashing against the huge basalt boulders of the river bed, pounding against the shiny cliffs eight hundred feet below you. But there is no visible hint of river and the sound is a murmur no louder than the sound of blood circulating in your ears. It seems to reach you through your feet, as the subterranean muttering of Mother Earth herself.

It's a sensation that sticks in the memory, this listening to the planet. And it's one of the places which makes this country a Holy Land for me.

Frank Waters remembers such places. In the living room of the old house in Arroyo Seco where he has lived for forty years, and grown old, and written many of the books that illuminate the cultures of the Southwest for all the world, he told me about two of them.

Horse skull decorates an adobe wall near Chimayo.

One is that narrow peninsula of stone jutting southward out of Third Mesa, east of Oraibi. Every fourth year at the beginning of the Wu'wuchim ceremonial, on "The Night of the Washing of Hair" when Hopi young people are initiated into the most important Hopi religious kivas, the kachina spirits gather at a shrine under the cliff here. It is the assembly point from which they enter the villages to take part in the ceremonials. "There is something about that place which is difficult to talk about in rational terms," Waters told me. "I simply sense the spirit of the place—a holiness which makes you feel reverent."

A crossroads of history and pre-history, El Morro National Monument east of Zuni has served as a stone bulletin board for passersby for centuries. The sandstone bluff rises two hundred feet above the surrounding plain and has a spring at its base. The first written inscription carved in its cliff was done by Juan de Onate. On his way back from an exploratory trip from the Rio Grande to the Gulf of California, Onate carved "Passed by here the Adelantado Don Juan de Onate, from the discovery of the Sea of the South, the 16th of April, 1605." Long before Onate, Indians carved their petroglyphs and painted their pictographs on the cliff. And since, it has collected hundreds of inscriptions, memorials and notations, which make it a uniquely rich resource for historians.

The ruins of Awatovi speak in a sadder voice to Waters and it, too, is associated with Wu'wuchim. You reach it by driving south of Keams Canyon across to the southern edge of Antelope Mesa. At the close of the seventeenth century, Awatovi was one of the most important of the Hopi villages, a rival to Oraibi in authority and in the power of its religious societies. It was the home of perhaps eight hundred people; the base of the Arrowshaft Clan; and of elements of the Badger, Eagle, Sun, Tobacco and Parrot clans. Spanish records and Hopi legends tell us that in 1700, a Franciscan missionary named Juan Garaycoechea arrived at Awatovi. Before he left, he had converted seventy-three of its people to Christianity. Tapolou, a religious leader of the Sun Clan, worried that this defection from the traditional rites was destroying the power of Hopi ceremonies. Tapolou met with religious leaders of the other villages and argued that Awatovi and its people must be totally destroyed. Warriors from Oraibi, Shongopovi, Mishongnovi and Walpi slipped into Awatovi at night while the men of the village were in their underground kiva preparing for Wu'wuchim. They pulled up the ladder and slaughtered the trapped Awatovians with a rain of arrows, finishing off any possible survivors with bundles of burning greasewood thrown through the roof hole. Except for a few women and children parcelled out for adoption into other villages, everyone in Awatovi was massacred. Walls of its houses were knocked down and its grinding stones and pottery broken. When J.W. Fewkes excavated the village in 1892, he reported to the Smithsonian Institution that he found "the earth was literally filled with bones..." Fewkes said he was deterred from further excavation of a kiva "by the horror of my workmen at the desecration of the chamber."

Horses socializing on a San Juan river ranch and chiles drying at Nambe.

*Still-thriving San Felipe Pueblo beside
the Rio Grande and the abandoned
settlement on a nearby cliff* (right)
*suggest an answer to the mysteries
posed by ruins everywhere. The
legends of the Pueblo people, from
Hopi to Taos, teach that the vanished
Old Ones were their ancestors.*

Betatakin huddles under an overhanging cliff of Tsegi Canyon in the Navajo National Monument. Tree-ring dating shows this remarkably well-preserved village was begun in 1250, completed in 1286 and abandoned about 1300.

Hopi legends tell us its residents paused there on their long migration toward the Hopi villages. Hopis maintain a shrine below the ruins.

Waters lived three years with the Hopi while preparing his classic *Book of the Hopi*. He knows them better than any other white, loves their culture and understands the terrible scar this atrocity left on the memory of a tribe which — for very good reasons down a thousand years — has earned the right to call itself "The Peaceful People." For Waters, the site of Awatovi is a haunted place.

"You stand there, and think about what happened and you feel it weighing you down," Waters said. "The presence of sorrow."

Another of these haunted places is Bosque del Apache, the once-marshy Rio Grande bottom south of Socorro. Now it is a federal wildlife refuge. Winter brings the waterfowl and the waterfowl bring the past.

On those short, dark days, dawn appears almost due east, a glow lighting the sky behind the San Andres Mountain. Soon the sky is luminous. The slopes of the San Mateos take shape in the darkness, and the Black Range, and the Gallinas to the north. The Rio Grande is almost dry this season, the water which will pour down it in the spring being stored in mountain snow packs. But in the calm of the start of day you can hear the slight sound of the moving water, and perhaps the faint growl of a late-running truck on the interstate miles away. Wait a moment and you will hear something else, a sound made rare by civilization.

On the shallow, marshy ponds the snow geese are awakening; first a single voice, then another, and then a

Pictures carved into the boulders converted a prehistoric hunting camp into an art gallery at Petroglyph State Park near Three Rivers, New Mexico. In the background (right) rise the Sacramento Mountains, home of Apache mountain spirits.

scattering that swells into a concert. They awaken the Canada geese, and the multitude of ducks: the canvasbacks, mallards, buffleheads, pintails, shovelers, mergansers and mudhens. Far across the ponds another sound emerges now — the odd, piping one-note call of the greater sandhill crane.

The Apaches who made this cottonwood grove their camping place and gave it its name when Western civilization was still somewhere far over the horizon must have heard morning music like this. But that was generations ago, before shotguns made the migration routes down from the Arctic nests death traps for a billion birds. It is a sound out of tune with the Aspirin Age.

*Long House and the Cliff Palace,
among the most dramatic of the Mesa
Verde's Anasazi ruins, were abandoned
at the end of the thirteenth century
and rediscovered on December 18,
1888, when ranchers Richard Wetherill
and Charles Mason rode up the
canyon.*

Wait just a moment and your eyes will confirm what your ears are telling you — that you have travelled backward to a time before the human species ravaged the planet. The sky is streaked with red and yellow behind the Oscuras now, and the reflected color has turned the treeless slopes of the San Andres into folds of pale velvet. In the dim light, great patches of the ponds seem frozen and covered with patches of snow. But the snow is the white feathers of geese — more than fifty thousand of them when I visited last winter, and ten thousand Canada geese, and more thousands of cranes. Suddenly, in groups and patches, they begin to rise. A snow goose is big, wingspan up to five feet, and noisy. The concert of awakening birds becomes a roar of wings, a bedlam of bird calls.

I don't think it is possible for anyone who is in any way sensitive to beauty and the power of nature to stand under the bare cottonwoods beside the Bosque del Apaches marshes and watch the breakfast flight of its winter birds without being overpowered by what the eyes and ears receive. Overhead, the sky fills with wings — V after irregular V of white geese, the smaller formations of the darker, bigger Canada geese — a hundred hurrying squadrons of ducks and their myriad waterfowl cousins. The sun is rising now and some formations sweep high enough to be caught in the light, dazzling against the dark morning sky. The San Andres slopes, grey velvet now, form a backdrop for the kaleidoscoping birds. Overhead you see formation above formation above formation, and between the geese, the stately grey lines of sandhill cranes. The dawn display surrounds you, engulfs you, excludes the world of trucks on Interstate 25. Nothing exists but the sight and the sound, the musical conversation of birds and their wheeling patterns — white against blue. This is how it was a long time ago.

Clan symbols, abstractions, stick-figure portraits and depictions of game animals decorate the lava cliffs on Albuquerque's West Mesa.

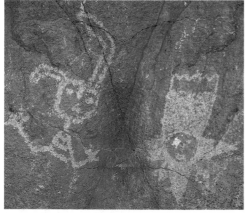

Patterns . . . of the Navajo Irrigation Project on the Blanco Plateau east of Farmington and an abandoned open-pit uranium mine near Grants, New Mexico.

The old and the new in volcanos are demonstrated by Cabezon Peak over-looking the Rio Puerco Valley and Sunset Crater east of Flagstaff. Cabezon is the core of a volcano that erupted in the Cenozoic Age, perhaps ten million years ago. With its ash and cinder cone worn away by eons of time, only the molten rock that once boiled in its center now remains.

According to Navajo legend, it represents the head of Yei'itso, *the first of the monsters killed by the mythical hero twins as they purged the Land Between the Mountains of the evil that infested it. Cabezon's sheer cliffs rise two thousand feet over the valley floor.*

Ancient juniper in Arizona's Walnut Canyon.

Ruins left by the Sinagua culture at Tuzigoot National Monument, Arizona.

*The Citadel Ruins at Wupatki
National Monument, Arizona, a for-
tified apartment house built atop a
table of basalt.*

Erosion exposes a flaking upthrust of sandstone in volcanic fields in the Wupatki National Monument.

Far to the northwest, beside the "stern" of Shiprock, one can experience an even more drastic adventure in time travel. In geological terms, this is a "ray," one of several that radiate outward for miles from the towering central core of the volcano. The same volcanic pressures that pushed boiling rock upward to form the volcano's core also cracked the earth's crust. Through these fissures, superheated magma pressed upward, like toothpaste from a tube, into the deep layers of ash the eruption had deposited. The same millions of years of wind and rain that eroded the volcano's cone and exposed Shiprock's black spires also cut away the ashes here and left these rays naked to the wind. They are twenty or thirty feet high in places and only two or three feet thick, and they wander for miles across the prairie, like thin and aimless Chinese walls.

Navajo Route 33 crosses a break in this ray on its way from U.S. 666 to Red Rock and the Kam Bihghi Valley. One late autumn day, I pulled off the road there and walked toward the spire, following a little-used path running along the talus slope below the wall. An early breath of storm was pushing down out of Utah that day. Here and there, chunks of the igneous rock had fallen out of the wall, leaving holes through which the north wind sang. Redtail hawks, big as golden eagles, hunted rodents over the prairie. A little sandy-colored prairie falcon was patrolling the wall itself, calling "key-key-key" in its piping voice. Miles to the south, Table Mesa stood on the horizon like an immense aircraft carrier anchored in a sea of blowing grass.

At Wupatki, a boulder too large to be moved became part of the structure.

To the Hopis, these mesas are the Center of the Universe, the goal of mythic migrations that led the clans who make up this tribe from their point of emergence to the four corners of the world, then back to their destined homes on the south end of Arizona's Black Mesa. Shongopovi (right), perched on the narrow ridge of Second Mesa, was settled by the Bear Clan, the first of the villages. The Fire Clan, arriving later, was assigned the site of Walpi on a spur of First Mesa. Inset is a portrait of Charles Loloma, one of the best-known of the Hopi artists.

Deer dancers, sticks representing the forelegs of the animals they imitate, re-enact one of the stories of the Nambe people's emergence from the womb of Mother Earth—from the time before the world of men lost its power to speak to the world of animals.

At the St. Francis Holiday ritual dancers circle in the plaza at Nambe in a recreation of an episode from a hunting myth.

The many kivas of Pueblo Bonito, in Chaco Canyon National Monument northeast of Crownpoint, New Mexico, are one of the several reasons anthropologists speculate that this strange community of villages might have been a religious center. Bonito probably housed as many as a thousand residents in its four-story structure. Since the area had other similar "towns" and hundreds of smaller settlements, the number of burials discovered seem far too few for the usual residential community. Farming experts also believe its peak population was far greater that its fields could have fed.

A network of roads, unnecessary for a society which had neither horses nor the wheel, lead out from the Chaco Wash ruins toward other Anasazi settlements across the San Juan Basin.

Another look at Pueblo Bonito. According to Navajo mythology, the people who lived here were enslaved by Always Wins, a supernatural gambler. The Navajo spirits Wind Boy, Darkness Boy, Growling God and others won their freedom by cheating Always Wins in a series of games.

First of all, Shiprock takes me back to the times of myth. The Navajos call it *Tsae-bidahi*, the Rock With Wings, rate it among their most sacred landmarks and forbid mountain climbers access. It was climbed in mythical times by the Monster Slayer, who learned from Spider Woman how he could reach the nest of the Winged Monsters. On the peak he killed the great birds. Then he taught their hatchlings not to hunt Earth Surface People but to become the eagles and the owls instead. Standing beside this wall of frozen grey lava reminds me of that. And then I find myself trying to imagine how it must have been when this wall was molten, glowing yellow with heat. How much force does it take to crack open the skullbone of the planet for miles in a dozen directions? How much to push that soaring black cathedral of stone (twenty stories taller than the Empire State Building) up from the prairie? I try to imagine the sound—like trying to imagine ten thousand hydrogen bombs exploding. I try to imagine the heat when that immense upthrust was the boiling throat of a volcano. I fail, of course. But trying puts time, and man's works, and me in a different perspective.

Those of us in whom stark and lonely places cause a rising of the blood can find many of them on the Colorado Plateau and in the eroded desert country that forms its southwestern margins. Another such place for me is the floor of Canyon de Chelly below the White House ruin.

The water flows clear, cool and shallow over the flat sandy bottom here. I am one who grew up barefoot, prowling creek bottoms for those fantastic things that country boys hunt. For a man who has survived beyond middle age, finding a place to re-experience, without loss of dignity, the childhood sensation of cold water on bare ankles and clean sand between the toes isn't easy. This stream bed has the perfect privacy anachronistic waders require. It even offers the spurious excitement of spots of quicksand—places where your feet move across a stream bottom that quakes and sucks, threatens to engulf and recalls all those scary old boyhood myths.

Pueblo del Arroyo began about 1030, more than a hundred years after the construction of Bonito. It featured an unusual circular structure with three concentric walls, the purpose of which must have been ceremonial.

This tree trunk beam, like others that supported the roofs of Chaco Canyon apartment houses, must have been carried some fifty miles from the pine-fir forests in the Jemez Mountains to the east, or the Chuskas to the west.

The Aztec Ruins in the valley of the San Juan River at Aztec, New Mexico, is one of many such sites that seems to have links with Chaco.

Above the treetops, the Anasazi ruins that give the place its name seem small. The sandstone cliff soars above them toward a sky that is unreasonably blue. The cliff dwarfs the ruins, and the cottonwoods, and me. Leached minerals carried by seepage has left them streaked and stained in vertical patterns that suggest whatever your imagination bends them to suggest. And here and there on the walls is the work of human artists, the pictographs and petroglyphs left by the Old Ones who lived here once and went away. In a shady place sheltered from the sun, I find the figure of Ko'kopilau, the humpbacked flute player, painted on the stone. Here he is depicted walking, his flute a straight line drawn down from his mouth, hump round with the seeds he scattered in the times of myth. Hopis of the Flute Clan still sometimes sing his song, but it is so incredibly ancient that no one remembers the meaning of the words.

When the breeze is almost still, I think you can still hear Ko'kopilau's music here if you really listen. But perhaps it is the bells worn around the necks of the Navajo sheep. The echo of the cliffs converts their multiple tinkle into something that sounds like Pan's reed pipes.

You could make a litany of the names of such Holy Places: Lime Ridge country northeast of Mexican Hat; the pyramid shape of Dzilintsan Peak, where the Navajo Black God lives on Black Mesa; Hole-In-The-Rock country on the Escalante River arm of Lake Powell; the Vermilion Cliffs towering over the Colorado River below Lee's Ferry. All of them and scores of others remind me of the advice N. Scott Momaday gave to his readers in *The Man Made of Words*. He told us we should all spend a little time concentrating our minds upon the remembered earth, upon some particular landscape. Man, Momaday told us, ought to "look at it from as many angles as he can, to wonder about it, dwell upon it. He ought to imagine that he touches it with his hands at every season and listens to the sounds that are made upon it. He ought to imagine the creatures that are there and all the faintest motions in the wind. He ought to recollect the glare of noon and all the colors of dawn and dusk."

Spider Rock in Canyon de Chelly National Monument, Arizona. Now the summer grazing ground of Navajo flocks, its canyons once were home for Anasazi farmers.

The great de Chelly and del Muerto canyons of the monument were cut by water draining out of the Chuska Mountains to the east. The runoff wore through the hard Shinarump conglomerate formation on the surface and then eroded the softer de Chelly sandstone. The nature of this erosion caused many of the protective overhangs that attracted cliff dwellers throughout the Southwest.

As I visit these holy places, dwell upon them, imagine them at every season, remember them in all their colors, I am reminded, too, of the Cheyenne story of creation:

In the Beginning, their origin story tells us, there was only Maheo, the Power. He looked around him and saw nothing, listened and heard nothing, felt, but there was nothing to feel. And so Maheo decided to form a Universe. In doing this he came to the moment when he held a ball of mud in the palm of his hand and created Earth. He decorated it with mountains, oceans, clouds, rivers, forests, lakes and meadows, with flowers, reeds, vines and grasses. He lit it with sun and moon, filled its air with birds, its waters with fishes and its forests with animals. And Maheo looked at what he had made and saw that Earth was full of beauty. He stared at Earth and fell in love with it. And so he created man and woman from his own body. It would be their duty, he told them, to care for Earth forever.

Dark streaks on the cliff faces look like dampness left by seepage but are actually "desert varnish" formed by thousands of years of mineral deposits. They were favorite canvases for the petroglyphs of Anasazi artists.

De Chelly Wash runs deep only during the spring snowmelt period and after torrential "male rains." Usually, its sandy bottom is a comfortable road used by the Navajos who occupy summer hogans along the stream.

The blue water of the San Juan River near the Navajo Dam, above Farmington, New Mexico.

*Steam of the Four Corners Power
Plant near Farmington.*

The Glen Canyon Dam near Page,
Arizona.

The Grand Canyon

A mule train on its long journey to canyon bottom.

A view of Monument Valley on the Arizona–Utah border.

Navajo moving sheep in Monument Valley.

*The muddy San Juan winds through
its goosenecked canyon near Mexican
Hat, Utah.*

Shiprock, the Navajo "Rock with Wings," seen down one of the great basaltic rays formed when lava squeezed upward through cracks in the earth crust. The monolith spires rise twenty stories taller than the Empire State Building. The Navajo Hero Twin, Monster Slayer, climbed Shiprock, killed the Winged Monsters and taught their hatchlings to become eagles and owls.

El Capitan, another of the ancient volcanic upthrusts that dots the Colorado Plateau, against a summer sky.

Monument Valley, afternoon and sunset.

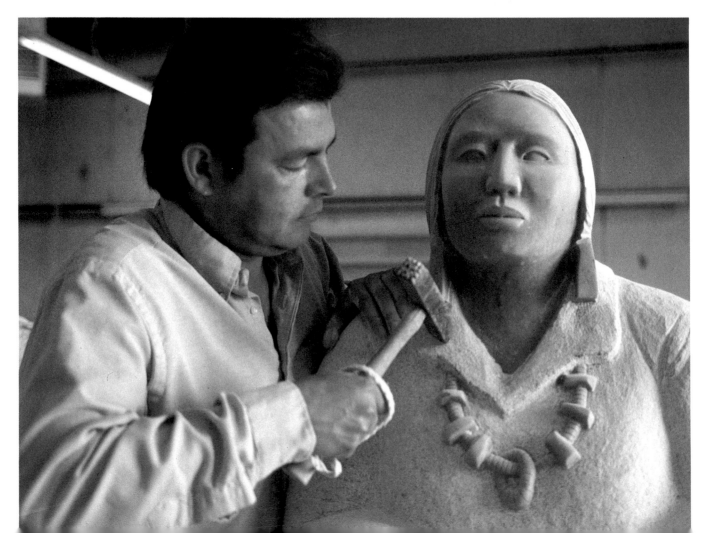

Santa Fe sculptors Doug Hyde and Agnes Sims.

*Galisteo sculptor
Allan Houser.*

Al Lostetter at work in his studio at Abiquiu.

Decorated skull at Tesuque, New Mexico.

An abandoned mine heading above Creede, Colorado . . .

. . . and a slag-heap of antlers from the Creede deer harvest.

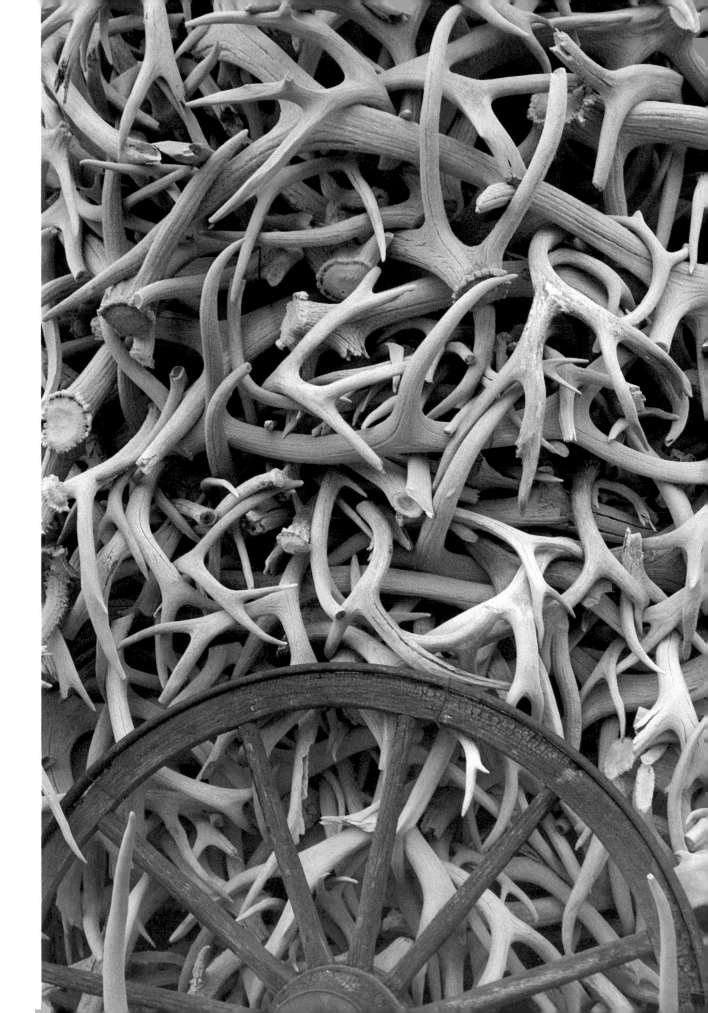

When these trees flourished in the
Petrified Forest of Arizona's Painted
Desert, what is now California was
deep under the ocean and the
Southwest was a low-lying plain
where meandering rivers flowed north-
ward through dense swamps. That
was two hundred million years ago, in

the Triassic Age. The forest and the dinosaurs who lived in it were buried under mud and volcanic ash, fossilized and uncovered by eons of subsequent erosion. Today, it has the world's largest array of petrified wood and one of its richest deposits of fossil plants and animals.

The Painted Desert deserves its name,
particularly in early morning and late
evening light, and especially after
summer rainstorms have washed its
dazzling variety of minerals free
of dust.

Bryce Canyon has been called one of the wonders of the world. And like the Grand, its marvels defy description, leaving the viewer speechless at such a demonstration of natural architecture: spires, walls, temples, castles, battlements, towers, steeples, niches and tunnels done in pinks, reds and yellows.

*Bryce Canyon's "Silent City"
formation . . .*

. . . mimicked by the white lines of late-autumn aspens on a Utah mountainside.

*Blooming rabbitbrush and bare
granite in Zion National Park.*

Saguaro National Monument outside of Tucson.

"Tipi" motel units at Grants, a snowy morning at Santa Fe's Inn at Loretto and the churchyard at Cañoncito, New Mexico.

". . . Finally, when Maheo was finished with creation, when the world was made, when his mind had created people, and the animals and birds and fish, then Maheo looked at what he had done and thought about his Power. I will make one more being, he decided. Something that could take the place of all the rest. And so Maheo, the Power, created buffalo."

—from the Cheyenne creation story

Béla Kalman

TONY HILLERMAN, of Albuquerque, New Mexico, is a life-long South-westerner, a former editor of *The New Mexican* at Santa Fe who then spent twenty years as a professor at the University of New Mexico. But he is best known for his novels about the Navajo Tribal Police and the sprawling reservation they guard in Arizona, New Mexico and Utah. Those novels are now published in fifteen languages and have won for him a national award from the U.S. Department of Interior, the Media award of the American Anthropological Association, designation as Grand-master of the Mystery Writers of America.

Hillerman is also author of many magazine articles about the Indian country of the Colorado Plateau, some of which are collected in *The Great Taos Bank Robbery*. He was editor, with the late Jack Rittenhouse, of *The Best of the West*, an anthology of letters, court records, sections of memoirs and docu-ments, and short fiction selected to illuminate the peculiar nature of the American West and of the people who inhabit its high, dry landscape.

BÉLA KALMAN (b. 1921 Budapest, Hungary) spent 35 years of his life in his native Hungary and came to the United States after the Hungarian revolution in 1956. He became a photographer after graduating from the Berzsenyi Gimnazium in 1939. Kalman received his master's degree in 1943 and opened his own studio in Downtown Budapest. In 1952 his studio was taken away by the state, and he spent five years working in a state cooperative. After a year in Chicago and in New York he settled in Boston and operated an advertising photography studio for 25 years. He retired from the 9-5 routine, and now he works on photographic books. His first book *Angkor* was published by Harry Abrams in New York. This book was first published in 1987, and two other books are in the works: *Jerusalem* and *Travels in Tuscany*. Kalman is a part time resident of Santa Fe. His works are in twelve museums, and in his 50 years in photography he has won numerous awards and medals and the lifetime distinction of Master of FIAP.

Paul Logsdon